So

Sequence of Love Poems

by

ROBERT PEEL

ROBERT PEEL

SONNETS

This Edition

First Published in 2009

By Non-Aristotelian Publishing

Isle of Man

ISBN No. 978-0-9510924-6-0

Published by Non-Aristotelian Publishing

Clifton, Slieu Lewaigue, Maughold, Isle of Man, 1M7 1BG

Printed and bound in Great Britain by
CPI Antony Rowe, Chippenham and Eastbourne

1. This series is dedicated to a certain idealized lady and others.

2 I dedicate this to Adam Peel, my son and friend.

3. Also my thanks to Ted Falconar for his interest and for many stimulating conversations and especially since my stroke.

4. My indebtedness to Jaccie Hamilton-Jones for all the help on the IT side.

5. And last, but not least, this sequence is dedicated to all lovers and poets who still believe that love means something in our lives. This is all I wish to say. Let the Sonnets speak for themselves.

Contents

SONNETS

First Series

Sonnet 1 (Dance)

Ah, yesterday, I held her in my arms.

The normal dance was carefree no-touch twist.

I asked, she rose, we met in waltz's charms.

Then all at once, we both were wrapped in mist.

Our hesitant feet .... observed with stress,

A sensitive hand .... felt thrillingly

The shimmering skin .... through flimsy dress

She pulled me right close .... so willingly.

A magic moment suddenly occurs

We stare at each the other's stare. Time stops.

The wonderment is neither mine nor hers,

But universal in its scope. Guard drops.

Our locking eyes in brilliant dancing beam

Arouse an ageless boundless waking dream.

Sonnet 2 (First Kiss)

Today, viewed afresh, we found time and space
To be alone together for a while
She paused then nearing gently stroked my face.
Pressed calm was devastated by her smile.
Our lips just met in crazy tight exclusion
Non-expert mouth gave promise bitter-sweet
I broke reserve to break naive confusion;
Electric shocks then shook me to my feet.
I'm hers, I'm hers, I'm hers, for evermore,
I do not care how much I'm bound or wrecked.
All limited affairs that went before
Did not prepare me for such stun-effect.
A simple thing, a tentative embrace,
Has set receptive hearts on life-long race.

Sonnet 3 (Moorland)

Love-smashed I drifted out of town today
To shout aloud at trees and fields; on, on;
On to moorland cloud-heart-reflected grey,
And yelled out my frustration; she's gone, gone;
This weekend separation, I can't stand.
But hold, though absent love is hard to bear;
Lie back, stare at the sky, soak in the land,
Breathe in the air, think of her cool, prepare.
Beyond her rim capacity to fire
The blood inside my veins to laval streams,
Much more than common physical desire
She's roused prolonged and elevated dreams:
Darling; now, eternal; reverse the trend;
The need of body, love and soul; no end.

Sonnet 4 (The Senses)

It's time we sealed our love; disguise it not,
In latent disarray of passion's smart;
The romance cannot last its present lot;
In crumbling temple, headstrong weakened heart;
The ecstasy we both can see, recall;
In echoing impulsiveness outsprung;
My heart-throb hold the heart-beat and enthral
The gathering bemused when it's outsung;
It's time, my love, it's time, my love, you know
To go exaggerate the gentle touch
That you and I delight in down below;
For never should we disengage as such.
Then all you taste and smell and hear and see
Ingest my love; and leave the feel to me.

Sonnet 5 (Waterlilies)

I feel the tingling throb of growing young

Enticing search for physical expression

Beneath my hands, and hear the softly sprung

Beseeching call for masculine aggression

Invade my inner ear. "Give me to me,"

Your eyes so grave intone, "Please soothe contusion

Of loneliness." So I absorb your plea,

And soul to soul we seek harmonic fusion.

But much to our discomfort and dismay

We cannot find the courage to explore

The full extent of stirring love's display

In sheets of waterlilies. Shut the door.

Though Earth and we may lose that love tonight,

You must agree our union seeking's right.

Sonnet 6 (Novices)

We tentatively lie in novice bed
Enwrapped in self-exploring willing feeling
Emerging surge to heightened plane. Instead
Her probing fingers find my mind, revealing
A harsh exploding naked sheet of light;
My curious stroking, stoking furnace gleam,
Extracts an all-embracing sigh so tight
Yet loose erratic heart-beats break the dream;
The virgin needs; erotic love refused
To expedite our striving searching. Drawn
Apart, our love is once again confused
With moon and roses, scented rainfall, dawn.
Then clumsy innocence and pain take hold
There's achievement, remorse, shyness, hot, cold.

Sonnet 7 (Broken Dusk)

Throughout her breaking dusk his love cries out

"I've found your happiness in me -- impressed."

He laughs to find it true, and has to shout,

"Mould it, hold it, hard inside the breast.

"If sturdy love should fail, the heart will die.

"Fire me, tire me, form a pure delight."

Her glowing ardour causes her to cry,

"Take me, make me soar in heightened flight."

Below the crescent moon her love sighs clear,

"Rush me, crush me, fast inside your soul,

"You took me into space unknown; lost fear."

They rest in limb-locked coda-light -- a whole.

"Refine their love," the dawn-sun seems to say,

"I'll hold them now forever or a day."

Sonnet 8 (Nothing)

Nothing in my life prepared me for this
Nothing -- no English novel of romance
No Radha-Krishna songs could promise bliss
No film, girl-chat, nor males observed askance.
O bosom friend, you ask me how I feel.
Are there words to utter utter emotions?
Just talking so increases his appeal
That pools of gold explode to glowing oceans.
His maleness fascinates -- envelopment
In space -- his strong incensed kind hands run warm
As roses rouse my full development
Acute, rich sky-blue eyes black thoughts can storm.
Love has lost its gravity, o rejoice,
The nuggets float through his melliferous voice.

Sonnet 9 (Regaining Rhythm)

I tried to sing a song about my lover

Of last night. Music failed me. The bright air

We composed vanished. I could not recover

The rhythm I had thought I had had there.

This morning found me over a bed, full

Of bright petals. I saw them blooming. Fresh

Shadows spread fast across them all to pull

The eyes away, a dark elusive mesh.

In fiery afternoon my brain cajoled

Itself to conjure up a painted theme

About my darling love my lustred gold

Within the afterglow of passion's gleam.

Absorb the canvas dream within your pen

Transmute her spell to view in sonnet ten.

Sonnet 10 (Portrait)

A dusky reverie confronts me, trembling.
I'll tell the world about the fascination
My love holds over me. An urge resembling
Proudness attempts to mould the fragmentation
Of your illusive form into a wholeness.
But why try to portray an illustration
So amazing? I ask myself with drollness.
Just flash out snips to make you *the* sensation;
The laugh a shimmer of pure sound, is splendour;
Your teeth so white and even; slim-line fingers
Of lotus hands, whose grip is hard yet tender;
Caressing eyes, intense, their magic lingers.
Your svelte sublim .... I've reached the end so fast,
Again your essence has been overpassed.

Sonnet 11 (Toast)

We meet this morning, sun-lit, riding high,
As love it seems has now forgotten crying,
All happiness resides in lover's sigh;
Relaxed; we can ignore external prying ....
Eyes; gaze beneath the surface charm; bloom-shine;
That lustrous laughter-flow, a sparkling lure
That dancing, bubbling, springing rising wine;
Well down to catch the vineyard essence pure;
Not love profane; but chivalry past thrust
Immersion driven through its liquid scent
The depths; not sprung in champagne's sparkling; must
Exclude intoxication of intent.
Now, raise your glasses to your crystal stars
The Milky Way is drunk behind wine bars.

Sonnet 12 (The Game)

We're caught within romanticism's court
As we attempt a matchless love affair.
"Love all," exclaims our Eros voice so taut
So we begin the game beyond compare.
You serve me notice to observe surprise,
On downward swerve I move to catch the sally
To counteract the awe-filled counter sighs
That make us stretch to end our strokeful rally.
Within the game of love we have reduced
Each other's bounds to bind the other's way,
And take advantage equal sets induced
To break ties' weakness. Yet we both cry, "Stay!"
This is no game when all is said and done,
We are unmatched because no-one has won.

Sonnet 13 (Laugh)

Till now our love has been a serious wondrous

Affair, ecstatic, secret, all too new,

I guess we felt we'd hear delirious thunderous

Applause, amazing, natural sound in hue,

Yet certain doubts tense tautened nerves this Spring

To fiddling point, so gut reaction fears,

O yes, can damp our shaded ardour, bring

The bower down, with claps, about our ears.

Who cares? Today you laughed without a care

Full flights of rippling liquid; angels grounded;

Cadenza, purity without compare,

Heart warming, merriment makes me dumbfounded.

I thrill to hear appealing peals trill fast

While present laughs at future flailing past.

Sonnet 14 (Questions)

Can we withstand such intensity, is
It possible to tolerate such heat
Beyond sun-bursts within corpuscled fizz
Sizzling through teeming rain in turmoiled beat?
Do we expect dreams, in our vanity,
To endue us with abilities; say;
Beyond bounds of reason and sanity;
To nurture unreality each day?
How is it scoffing killjoys cannot kill
Our appetites for love enthusiastic,
That despite consuming passion we still
Can manage to remain so chiliastic?
How love survives we should not have to wonder
Our duty lies in circumventing blunder.

Sonnet 15 (Queen of the Night)

Close your eyes, my love, dispel the sun-spell
That searing light that haunts your searching brain.
Close your lips, my love, repel the thought-swell
That will bemuse or twist our love so plain.
Let mysteries of moon-light guide our trail
To ecstasy, fulfilment, merely us.
Let silken aura sprayed through love prevail.
In truth let common sense command -- no fuss.
Your rat-ki-rani stirs in midnight shift.
Desires no more, no less, than please you here
And now. Please pleasure me my darling, drift
In swirl of scent all lovers do revere.
Accept the coolness spun by moon replete,
Which we alone can fashion into heat.

Sonnet 16 (Body and Soul)

That's right! I rave or write about affairs
Concentrated on the physical side
Of things, about a bout, about a fight
Sweet tussled contact. We're electrified
By action and reaction to love's flares.
It does not matter morning, noon or night
Thought's preoccupation's deep skin delight.

That's wrong. A sudden intense flash of fire
Illuminated corners of the mind
Untouched by current generated scheme
And exposed love more genuine than blind
Beauty or that which relies on desire.
It's immaterial; really extreme
Incorporeality; lust must dream.

Sonnet 17 (I Love You)

Let me exclaim; I love you; will persist

In doing so despite their claims I'm boring.

Yes, at first your magnet eyes, lips like mist,

Open arms, open legs, spring softness roaring

Down arteries was sole preoccupation

Of youthful ardency, and breaking through

To centres of excellence, fascination

Of you, of me, both maybe. I love you.

A blink at eternity, crows may dance,

Your legs may close; my heart is ever wide

Open. A touch, one word, nuance, close glance

Is all you'll need to hold me by your side.

I love you, will continue evermore.

Trite, you say? Truth requires no ornate score.

Sonnet 18 (Kiss)

Open the door. Let us enter and kiss.
The walls of my heart absorb these soft gold
Shimmering sun drops. What heavenly hiss
Of jealousy as young love warms the old.
Should our passion reflect true knight in armour
Listful in courtly love, yet rutting wenches?
Shall we, ovine in pastoral, greet a charmer
With beats of pleasure when our sheep maid blenches?
You tease me quoting Indian censor's ban;
No lip caress, not screened. Perhaps they're right.
Would animated Khujeraho make man
Or woman beautiful or ugly sight?
Uh. Who cares? Day and we are young before
Night struggles through to us. Kiss me once more.

Sonnet 19 (Light Ship)

I ply a dangerous course by writing so
My paltry lines on love, to heave and fake (near)
Them: Petrarch, Dante, Michaelangelo,
Sidney, Spenser, Daniel, Drayton, Will Shakespeare.
What steers the man to wake the greats this way
When modern flights invite him to expose
Himself in high flown plane? All I can say,
Restriction, taut in rhyme and metre, flows
The vessel through love's rip-tide passioned swirls;
Controls anarchic thought within its craft.
Undisciplined *verse libre* whips and whirls
Ideas, elevating airy waft.
Have patience reader, listener, lover do,
Our light ship holds a beam for her, me, you.

Sonnet 20 (Love is dead ....)

A living tradition snorts, "Love is dead
"In the arts. (And in life too?). Then for sure
"The sonnet form's a fourteen poster bed
"Overpropped dead-old dust bag. What a bore!"
A dormant tradition breathes, "Love is dead
"Against our anarchistic temporal trend
"Here today, gone tomorrow, past is said
"To be or not to be. Fashions can end."
My loving tradition utters, "Love's dead
"On time, whichever zone you fix, and hums
"Sublimely through soft hearts, be they closed spread,
"Young, old. Bold arts, please, make it as it comes."
The public mutter, "Does it really matter?"
I claim: "Love thrives despite your bedlam patter."

Sonnet 21 (Dawn Walk)

Side by side we amble away from night;
Done now. Breaking sun casts bronze dawn-long hymns
Across waking fields, heart entrancing flight.
There's spring in the air and spring in our limbs.
The occasional brush of word, eyes, arms
Is a comfort secure, even supreme.
No need for much speech, we feel through our palms.
We leave chitty chatty to birds' full stream.
Not a shimmer of leaf, so calm the air
So still risen morning, still our hearts bright
Burst into dayshine, no fluttering there,
Intense is the feeling and April light.
So let us enjoy the dawn while we may
Between .... heat of the night, heat of the day.

Sonnet 22 (Exclamations)

O, Urvasi, you ask me to describe
Love. Ah! Who can say? I'm sure not me! No,
I don't have that way with words, can't inscribe
A monumental piece on love with show.
The ecstasy, the wonderment is there
For me to feel; the tightening of sense
Expansion of inner self. I declare!
It seems no other's life's been so intense!
You see, my feeling far surpass my skill
In writing these few words yet I do hope
You'll understand this stupefying thrill,
Outrushing soul, beyond my verbal scope.
Dear bosom friend. That's all. Please, pardon me.
Just know that love's the greatest play. You'll see!

Sonnet 23 (Heartlines)

It's curious: I've known you in full flow,

In full-flowered bed of blooming desire;

So barely bearable; yet your skirt's slow

Swirl pulls heartlines, thus raising passions higher.

Incredible: although you do arouse

Down softness through night's familiar spell;

Yet hardly hardening; the brush of blouse

On cheek has its own charmed sensual swell.

A grave belief: at the altar of love

No sacrifice is too great for love's sake;

Happy happenstance; a pure voice above

Carnality rejoins puerile heart's break.

So, Darling, it seems whatever you do

Simple, coy, innocent, makes me love .... you.

Sonnet 24 (Although)

Although Love's course has coursed through veins for ages,

And we've read poetry on love in past

Same love we chase through life-streams, love that rages

Around our hearts, leaves bystanders aghast;

Although the world and we know otherwise

Each liaison seems passionful unique

And constantly eyes open in surprise

As each pair scales what seems unconquered peak;

Although the trendy claim that love's old hat

That it has all been done and said, it had,

(That we should quietly announce, "That's that,")

And scorns love and/or poetry as sad;

Yet, our affair and my sincere portrayal

Will not allow a facile glib betrayal.

Sonnet 25 (What can I say?)

What can I say that's not been said before?

Ought I presume our love is so unique?

All my questions you (listeners)/(readers) might ignore

For surely you are wrapped in self-mystique?

Should I compare you to a Summer.......or

Beauty, sweet Love, is like the morn;......they speak

In voices dear to me, their language sure;

Phil's Stella; love me for love's sake ....: What cheek,

What cheek, that I invoke sound pictures from

The past! I need not. She and I are just

As sound. I only lack that much aplomb

To set our love on par with those out-thrust.

Although it's all been done and stated erst

Our love, like blooms, is as fresh as the first.

Sonnet 26 (Joy)

The joy of creation; the whole world's sigh

Floods my opened being, exquisite sound;

Light-streams tumble down, drawn from anthemed sky;

By day, by night, my heart, my soul has found

The love of live earth; hurled through scented awe;

Attar of roses, dry dust rained, mown lawn,

(Bends Cupid's shafts, calms thunderbolts from Thor);

Dazzled by sea-gleam, stroked, sun-glanced, breeze-borne.

Love's brazen beams highlight singing trees' leaves

And butterfly-sheen. Hear bumble-bee zing-sips,

See drops of dawning dew bead spiders' weaves.

Feel feather-light thrill from whispering wing-tips.

Your touch, ecstasy, fragrance, laugh, eye-shine,

Your mind, empathy, goodness, love, all mine.

Sonnet 27 (Meteorites)

I should not forecast immortality

For you or love. That would be incorrect.

The oldest lovers in reality

Are lost in shifts of time; Doppler Effect.

Sight dies soon, sound's not far behind, the source

Of energy less frequently regales

Us with what's going on, and then of course

At full reception the final wave fails.

It's true that finity of thoughts can't cope

With magnitude of emotions I've got

Through intensity of love. Can but hope

That words released, like meteorites burn hot.

"Temporal love has its own rewards," you state.

Agreed, but artistry of love moves fate.

Sonnet 28 (Immortality)

Now, doubts intrude into the seasoned mind
That claims of immortality are wrong.
That words imparted, those of sequenced kind
May not be true to life, may not last long;
That, come what may, it may not be, it still
It might not be an evermore affair.
Just the thought that this is so tends to kill
Enthusiastic will to use ones flair.
These lines may run through dream-mined pitted mind-field
This page is dying to join the mortal coil
And listless love might shatter knight's declined shield
Then bury all beneath extracted spoil.
All fanciful predictions, linked with time
And death, die tonight, no rhyme or reason.

Sonnet 29 (Cedar)

The cedar etched against a star brushed sky
Absorbs warm silence leaving love stroked ground.
With barely touching shoulders you and I
Sit motionless in harmony; so sound.
The depth of stillness stills our souls on high
When night-enshrouded keepsakes drift around
To elevate this side of love profound.

Although this calm seems dull by fashion's ways
The slightest surface nick reveals, outcries
That love's yet friction-red like sappy days
But heightened by the evergreen's uprise
Above stark physicality's outblaze.
Deep harmonies from light and shade arise
Contrasting height with depth. What a surprise.

Sonnet 30 (Meltdown)

I kissed the sunrise of your mouth so tender
Scorn-laughed to death the savageness of time,
Was in my hands. I held a waist so slender
Absorbing thrillingly our love sublime.
Was meltdown through your midday heat of ardour
(Yet still escaping seconds trickled free),
We squeezed each other's torsos closer, harder,
For nothing mattered in our urgency.
You saw a violent sunset in my eyes
And realized the time had come to fly.
Kaleidoscopic fragments sliced the ties
Our tightened hearts have truly left to lie.
But wait, although we part in disarray
Our love, I'm sure, will never run away.

Sonnet 31 (Lament)

Why was I born, Fate, why at all a girl?

And now a woman, why with face so fair

With magic hands, velvet skin, breast of pearl,

And worst of all, with heart to love .... despair.

Five arrows fired from Kama's bow, bee strung,

Burst into multitudes of shafts of light.

My opened adult soul is much too young

To die yet -- so alive. Now is that right?

Why was I born, Fate, why at all a slave

To custom, passion, caste and man depressed?

My Eastern ties are stronger than the grave

Romantic love, read novel love's gone west.

Why was I born, Fate, why at all at all?

I cannot stand the freedom. Back I'll crawl.

Sonnet 32 (Flight)

Desolation. How has it happened that
I allowed her flight, did not fight to stop
Her? The jet ingests her. Funny -- heart's flat.
I see, hear, cannot feel. Batsman's hands drop.
Uh. Wrenching pain. Each blast of turbine sears
Skin, this morning stroked; sadly joked; I shriek
In silence, as plane screams away. Dry tears
Burn up eyes while it waits. Now engines peak
Dances up runway, lifts; soul shuts off; banks
Hard through broken cloud, shredded shroud. I twist
Handwave. Crow black despair. Haze through eyes blanks
Out outlines, wraps sec brain in permamist.
Though being's raison d'être fled this land
Life, forever missed, will go on and on and on and ....

Sonnet 33 (Lonely College)

Monsoon, with furied clouds burst scented dust
The streets become a flood, the lake a sea.
My first and only love, so soft in lust,
Is tied, marooned, no longer thinks of me.
He will return no more -- his life his own
And her (Who is she then?) I'd love to know,
And yet, I don't. My scattered love is blown
With tears which runnel cheeks to join rain's flow.
A woman I'm alone in this great college
To fellow people's loneliness I've fled.
The thunderous din of voices drowns out knowledge
Of season's brightness. I've become brain dead.
I was dying to live, when love prevailed
I am living to die now we have failed.

Sonnet 34 (Letter)

A letter flew across the seas to query
(I shudder chilled to think you thought of this)
Me, who my girlfriend was, was I so weary
Of loveless life since days of love-filled bliss.
Except you have beguiled by guileless charm
Such question should have drilled my nerves to shrill,
For countless missives, sent without a qualm,
Conveyed the hidden phrase: I love you still.
Sucking fear appals me now; I can't think.
That simple coded message had misled
My guarded anti-censor written jink
From openly affirming troth's misread.
Now love is buried deep in cryptic word
Internal truth must always lie interred.

Sonnet 35 (Beckoning)

So still you stand with hands on rounded hips
Your eyelids now half-draped to hide the sun,
You talk in silence through those moistened lips
And beckon me to join you, one to one;
Out there, now summer fullness is matured;
You breathe the sigh of bosom's fall and rise;
One yearns to gaze and needs to be assured
By eyes, molten, soft black smouldering eyes.
You know the love that flowered years before
Now urges me again to join with youth.
My India so inscrutably unsure
Did not reveal the element of truth.
And yet in contradiction it is true
The actuality of love is you.

Sonnet 36 (Go)

They say that absence makes the heart grow fonder
Perhaps they're right as he's a foolish lover
Brought to bay beneath full moon glare, to ponder
On love's long lost chase -- red heart's broken cover.
The pulse-beats slowed and stuttered as her fleeing
Through undergrowth of tangled yearned confusion
And stunted feelings, emphasised a being
Imagination blurred through its illusion.
No-no-no; sentimental thoughts will kill
The panting hart the running doe steel dead.
Go-go-go; action resolute may still
Let him slip the hunt, then catch her far ahead.
Reject the comfort drug of fearful sloth.
Jump to your feet, outrun the bounds, save both.

Sonnet 37 (*Saptapadi*)

Agni: straight god, marriage stage, who's a liar?

Faceless guests blind to Kama Dev. What next?

Oh where's love's flame? Throw rice in scented fire.

Dull-eyed betel-mouthed priest chants tedium text.

Rise, walk those seven steps. "Take one for force,"

My cool-voiced groom declares, "Two strength, three wealth,

"Four comfort, five offspring, six season's course,

"Seven as my friend." -- I marry in stealth.

Sita: do you hear? "Be faithfully true,

"May we obtain many sons." Womb's like putty.

"May they reach good age." Death take me in lieu.

Where is my true Ram? I'll perform iced Sati.

I remain silent -- always shall. Hold pain.

Servile wife until pyre. What will he gain?

Sonnet 38 (Broken Down)

He fretted through the eastern sky, planed jet,
To get to see her. He got there, got there.
Soul-bare, he brushed the haven of her hips
His half-turned back re-felt her finger-tips,
A final swift and stealthy stroke; not fair;
Declaring love, apology, regret,
And yet no hope. He lost the strength to prise
The ties that bound her: a nightmare, nightmare:
When care-worn-pain-filled fingers lost their grip
He half-turned back as he began to slip
Through sun-dead, moonlack, darkling, phantom air;
To stare past haunted caste-held clouded eyes:
She'd .... hid the harshness of rejection's glare:
He .... buffeted in jet stream of despair.

Sonnet 39 (Refrain)

Since we have sung the final song of love,
My lover, in this dark dark void; lack-breeze;
A stifled air; where cobwebs stretch above
Bowed heart-break; I must pull you off your knees;
Must join your broken dreams, must hold, must nestle
Your fevered head upon my bosom's rise,
To let my heart allow your strained ear wrestle
With fluttering sweet murmurings and sighs.
Beneath the pipal tree, shut-eyed, I'll pray;
Sit still and silent; absorb dark dark pain;
That festers deep in solitude; so may
Re-live the fading lay; past love refrain.
When dawn pales morning stars, we'll briefly gaze
At other's tears .... then drift on parting ways."

Sonnet 40 (Fever)

Heartless he lies in fever ridden train

Eye registers distorted time and space.

Flash past, slow down, down, down, inner tears drown.

Quick flick a switch: stay night or day light moon

Anon sense will plague the soul later soon.

Sole reality click clack up back down

Wheels on endless rails. Where is that face?

Lack luck, tick tock, the brain in mindless pain.

Cry dry tears, fly by fears, finite nears; what?

Hai, hai, hai, inner eye sees outward form.

It's cool up here floating calm. Go or not?

Time still speeds on its own track. Back to norm.

Now lower yourself love lover down low

Drift off to sleep despite the hypnopho.......................

Sonnet 41 (Strange Piece)

A score of years have passed since I have scored,

Have scored in staves, that love-song; past belief;

Have tried to play, but could not strike a chord,

Each prelude's been cut short by welled-out grief.

Ingenuousness I've tried, open heart,

Ingeniousness contrived, skilful craft,

And each attempt has tempted me to start,

To dash again to spill out fast a draft.

I cannot though, I cannot; deepened fear;

Each loveless counterpoint helps dull the theme

I cannot drown the cyclic taste of beer

Forever trapped in bar-backed pain. I'll scream.

Although somehow I've fuddled this strange piece

I know this start will not effect release.

Sonnet 42 (River Neb)

When bees do bicker over gorse shrubs sweet
Whose sultry scented flowers lull the mind,
When eyelids flicker through reflected heat
Off weir-scattered ripples, breeze designed,
When dragonflies do flit along our sight
Whose brittle slimness causes hearts to flare,
When fading cries of joyful youth skim right
Across the shimmer-skittered heat-hazed air;
Then, then my girl do we, with limbs entwined,
Absorb the broken images in brief
And in the swirl of field day lust will find
That hedge shade contact brings us light relief.
No aftermath from new mown crop will rise,
Uncomplicated harvest leaves no ties.

Sonnet 43 (Heavyweights)

Night. Besotted heavyweights were locked

In brawling mauling wrestled round affair;

The first manoeuvre for a grip skin shocked;

Stripped down entwined to their essentials bare.

A cross hand hold had had the bodies blocked

Without a light or artificial glare

A hip-lock brought a fall hit bottom rocked,

As bulging eyes have made a fruity stare.

Enclosing in the flesh began a cocked

Low one leg pick up inside trip set fair

To waist and ankle scissors ride upchocked

Then stalemate yielded each this lusty pair.

In arms companionship exhausted lay

The night of lust must rise to calmer day.

Sonnet 44 (Spring Storms)

Today our casual fling uplifted me.

A gentle spring storm in the Isle of Man,

The hail-shower spread before the vision, see

A slanting whitecap beaded curtain ran

Across the effervescent sky of brass.

The skittering drops on pavements, wet through,

Sounding like some shimmering beads on glass

Spangled us, slightly shivering anew.

And just as suddenly as it had started

It stopped, to let the clouds swirl far away.

The broken freshness, it and we imparted

To each other, cooled the enfevered day.

The quick release has made it for the hour

And parting holds no taste, not sweet nor sour.

Sonnet 45 (Soft-Porn)

In picture house bare copulation smacks

The eye with heavy clumsy stimulation,

Not thoroughbreds but sweating bangtail hacks

That churn out writhing boring simulation.

Can we observe obverse obscenity

When flesh on flesh presents us dirt cheap plonk?

Punch drunk we're staggered by its levity

Which rasps bad taste in aftermath of bonk.

At this late stage capitulations raise

In conjunction of bright stars (heaven-sprung),

The payers of bright play of love to blaze

Around delicious tussled courtship's tongue.

Draw a veil across the screen, let it be.

Act final scenes of love in privacy.

Sonnet 46 (Calcutta)

Cacophony, a mix of smashing sound
Invaded tiring minds already tipped
By shots in loveless arms. Torpid rage, ripped
By fired voices, volumes in to pound
The mashed up thought. And once again the round
Of horns, horns shriek, horns blast, horns, horns have whipped
The tiredness anew, to join the flipped
Out microphonics making pain rebound.

The silences of empty hearts now scorn
Amnesic skin thus forcing me to languish
Imploring for the quiet calm of night.
I've tippled alcohol on wounds forlorn,
Allowing them to merge in city-anguish.
Dear God, silent God, where's life's love's delight?

Sonnet 47 (Court-Piece)

Seven Down fever train, so long ago,

Dumped my out-bid heart inside a hot game

Of court-piece played in hovel's flicker flame,

When eyes and laugh asparkle touched me so.

Your surreptitious bosom, hand on show,

Flipped stroked and stroker. Flirtation -- no blame --

Was due to heart's debacle. All the same,

Decadle parting should have quenched the glow.

Your rushed appearance flushed out dormant madness

Tumbled down defenses like cardboard slump

Hard pressed suit, snatched, we've won again at sevens

And sixes. Your crucial hand gained, good heavens,

A caught peace, registered by thirteenth trump

The final trick collected fevered gladness.

Sonnet 48 (Branch Line)

Remember darling, how we mocked -- that day
In rattling local carriage courtship-bound --
The couple tense estranged, in silence wound,
Oblivious to all; he faced away;
Her eyes locked past us, inner hurt at bay;
How in our arrogance of love new-found
We nudge-scoffed eye-glance-pitied wedlock ground
To a halt. We would never go that way.

Recall, estranged love, mockery that flounced
On stress-filled faces, voices, gestures, eyes
That slowed our prattling laughter marriage, sliding
Towards a flat life finally renounced
With accusations, yellings, curse-mouthed lies
To grind to hate-filled locked-in court-bound siding.

Sonnet 49 (Son of Song)

A soughing breath of wind is emanating
From the heat-soaked land, and within its slow
Vortex smooth kites are swirling in the glow
Of sunlight, light debris specks, aggravating
The shimmered disturbance of the heart, waiting
For a swift stoop, down ray of hope, below,
For a life-enhancing movement to show.
Still, curling sigh of breath is elevating.

The ambitions of a hard, bright, entranced
Son of song enforced words through his skill
And skirled them out into the whirling world.
And through that trigger of release, the furled
Emotions spread their wings and have enhanced
The struggling poet's aim to strike at will.

Sonnet 50 (Joyful)

Joyful and jubilant my soul has woken.

After all those years dormant muse exploded

Inert monochromatic dreams of broken

Sleep, spurring into action my eroded

Heart: outdated, outcast, worn out, out-paced,

Rendered incapable of writing higher

Energetic, hard, flowing lines encased

Enchased with glowing words of flame, afire.

The apathy of inactivity

Ingrained by brooding hurt now runs through feeling.

Well, I accept new sensitivity

And henceforth I'll revel in love-revealing.

Right, be honest, if we had joined and wed

In time love would have spread, not penned instead.

Sonnet 51 (Memory)

A silken softness close on finger tips
A jewelled brilliance dancing in dark eyes
The touch of velvet texture on full lips
All hurled his seething doubts through cloudless skies.
The swaying sun warmed cooled emotion there
And flushed the heart of India's blood red rose
While whispering, cascading, brushing air.
Spectators sighed, "Her dusky skin it glows."
And never in the history of men --
Or so it seemed to them in heightened passion --
Could love like theirs be flattened out, but then
It was; it was defused by social fashion.
Now time has passed since surge-emotions raged
Their unfulfilled affair has been assuaged.

Sonnet 52 (Juhu)

He sees lookers-on hiding smiles inside
Their eyes, observing how an oldish hand
Will write of love and passion, which tide-slide
Like idols shaped on Juhu's beach of sand.
And he himself on seeing their reaction
Must with amusement wryly smile along,
And wonders if his voice has that attraction
To draw his audience out with lovers' song.
The pupal craft lay high-beached all these years
But after two decades it burst out free,
When it remembered laughter, love and tears,
To sing aloud to all of ecstasy.
Yes, it's just possible that relaunched flair
Will let him celebrate their love affair.

Sonnet 53 (Comfort)

They should not apportion blame, regret. No,

It would not be appropriate. They could

Study failure being useful to show

In general terms why, maybe, where they stood.

External forces far too great, were out

To thwart them; the disparity of race,

Enforced absences, fear of total rout

From caste and society. Can't lose face.

Internal forces not too great, were pure

Elaboration, fuddled clarity

Anxiety foolish immature

Would not let them grasp opportunity.

Yet, take this comfort both of us -- we must --

We join those famous love-affairs gone bust.

Sonnet 54 (Song Birds)

On haven isle in exile, self imposed,
Researching for expression, love declined,
As collared doves and nameless birds disclosed,
Wanton want of morals. He'd tried to find,
That love-lorn paragon within his breast
Without a cauterizing phoenix flame;
His song birds trilled their tunes of mortal jest
And finally he felt just .... no more blame.
Adonai not Adonis give him thought
Beyond resurgent bored eternal youth
That existential lovers can be brought
To everlasting nature of your truth.
Let myths flood past licentious Byblos' gore
Uncertainty of love haunts me no more.

Sonnet 55 (Heart Intact)

Time, you have done your hardest to destroy

Our love. Separation, silence, hard wedlock,

Aging, distance, all these did you employ.

No distraction even love out from bedrock

Offsprung enhances a purity of vision

Outshining light of day or outworn night.

An infinite resolve broke indecision

To bring the endless to an end all right

Left above-below, timeless void upending.

Perceived beyond through blinding cataract

A lightless formless entity descending

Down-up, up-down, revealing heart intact.

Time, you have done your hardest to destroy

Our love. Yet now I leap for very joy.

Sonnet 56 (Review)

Not now the fascination of warm flesh
Nor glimpse of hair cascading darkling rush
Nor waist so trim above those hips so fresh
Nor pouting lips that steal a damask blush;
That bloom of youth, *indica rosa*, grew
Millennial (as old as love?); no more;
That studded host of rose recurrent new
In arrogance men strained; again deplore
Its death. Do moderns scorn *ami du coeur*,
Preoccupied with fixed carnality,
And do they scintillatingly prefer
A bedded down .... instant "reality"?
Our love, that rose, blood-red in stolen dusk
Distilled itself, a re-found white-heart musk.

Sonnet 57 (Notes)

As these notes are perhaps in time not apt
To organize lost love -- yet -- love resounds.
Partial, whole, sad or glad; still, she astounds.
Her soul remains interred, beyond him, rapt.
These fractured tones in deathly silence, trapped,
It seems for aeons and aeons in mounds
Of stone, become enswathed in drunken sounds
Until the echoes, the echoes are lapped.

"Do your damndest time and death entwined."
Rejecting urgent dirge, compelling bond
Confirms we broadcast, universal air;
The theme, that sonnetry can spread beyond
Beyond itself and us and will declare:
"Their love and they have breathed out life refined."

Sonnet 58 (Sound Love)

This talk of Time and Death should not concern
Us now: Infinity's a Godknows day-
Dream: Why, Love is all powerful: Come, turn
Exilic hearts exhilaration's way.
Our foregone thens saw coming whens locked in
Present. Now, how about that? Love beats all.
Tight tolls of doom, decay, unbound they spin
In deadfast rhythms which lost souls enthral.
My dears, drop all ideas beside the now.
The past has run its course, the future will
Adapt itself to us, no fuss. Allow
Your heart to stroll through truth. We stand here still.
The Ring of Eternity is not round.
Its appeal whichever way is pure sound.

Sonnet 59 (Painted Lady)

What was that -- with Adonis on display;

Voluptuous Aphrodite, rose in cloud,

Skin, hair, lips, nails in colours worlds away.

Perfume assailed tight temple. Melted crowd

Allowed hips flaunting passage. Could she sway

The room; could they sway; what a pair; full proud.

Strip shroud. It's silicone gel, gelid stuffed

Firm jelly, overflowing nature's rise

To shadow belly, swell men's pride, all buffed

With skin-tone cream. Mascara taint-lens eyes

In dancelight fashioned model has us bluffed.

That compo creature self-moulds in her dies.

Painted lady, with unsurpassed veneer,

Plain beauty, my trim love, outstripped you clear.

Sonnet 60 (Taj Mahal)

Ethereal, that heaviness, white floating
Above darknesses of pain, mass uprising
Closing love with beauty, upraised by doting
Despot, prises viewers' eyes, so surprising.
His frenzied grief brought frenzied light creation
Detached from truth the marvel can be pretty
Beautiful; sun or moon-stroked stone formation
Formed in formaldehyde. Oh! What a pity.
Cold marble, whispered dome, built twenty years
Or more by thousands damned impressed endeavour.
Whose grief, whose toil employed, whose endless tears,
Whose thrall of passion should enthral forever?
My love no wealth no regal heights can claim
Yet reprints may outlast his marbled frame.

Sonnet 61 (Black and White)

That colourful enthusiasm's gone

That love no more is seen in local hue

The brilliance of horizon-stretching con

Exposing chroma voyage; fades from view;

The stark revealing wash of black and white

Has clarified the sharp-toned truth of our

Love, laid bare to all -- not a pretty sight.

I hesitate to use its focused power.

But even monochrome distilled ex-stream,

Now disappears within transparent sea

Conceived or served, an essence past our dream

Which still has not fulfilled its potency.

Evaporation catches light diffusion

So even this is not the real conclusion.

Sonnet 62 (Well well)

On going through this series once again
I must admit I wryly have to smile.
Confusion's dripped from out my black ink pen
So fact and fiction melded all the while.
It's been so long since I had truly started,
Much heart, emotion, sweat's in this creation,
That even I don't know when I've departed
From real life to realms of false elation.
Yet, underlying lying strands of pile
The thick underlay of truth should fare well
That's why the threadbare runner raised my smile
As constructive love's been laid up stair-well.
Now reader, since you've waded through this stuff
I hope you've separated smooth from rough.

Sonnet 63 (Farewell)

And now I write in naive simplest way
A codicil goodbye: God be with you.
I think I've written all I wished to say
About this love that's lasted us right through.
And now I doubt it hit a note eternal,
Reverberated consciousness sublime,
What reason for our injuries internal
All laid to rest without a death this time.
And now I've failed to reach the unattainable,
That perfect truth or perfect love in my
Imperfect world, my pitch is not sustainable,
Then I must close this work with coda-sigh.
Expiration done ....is tough;
Love's the stuff. Love's ....enough.

Second series

Half Score and Some
Rubicon Uncrossed
(Fractional Sonnet I)

Oh gem of fair morn, a flirt has been born;

She has just, today, ground her young way

Into my poor mind. I think I'll go blind

Drunk, in rock rock rock rock time. Jerky rhyme

Dominates spasmodic thought – brain cells, fraught

With inertia – headlighted rabbit – spelled in the habit

Of no mo..motion – and this time the juggernaut won't slow

Down, and people will observe, "The bugger bought it, serve

Him right; a pretender of the worst kind." Never mind-

Read me, dead or alive, you'll fail, strive

As you may. A frantic hand waves a wand.

Uh! There! Eye-rhyme has impelled itself. Catastrophe's dispelled.

My gem and I scuttle apart before being crushed under

                                       wheels of thunder

To enjoy our separate wondering ways. Happy days.

Her first flush of searching sex rose in cheeks
Is powerful with innocent immensity.
The first sparkle, highlighting auburn flecks
In her blue sky eyes, produce such intensity;
Skies of Spring, sprung waves wavering between
Heart's surge and hesitant crush-stirrings mingling
With control-thrill and young fear of unknown
Emotions; bright cornea-sheen; sense-tingling.
Between our eyes the years stretch in surreal
Skeins, and both our yearning undefined dreams
Interweave in feathered tangles that steal
Pale streaks across light flushing sunrise streams.
Generated by single touching finger
The generation gap eye-searches linger.............

**Then Die
Damp Eye
In the Sky
(Improper Fractional Sonnet II)**

Sonnet III
(Proper Sonnet)

Her eyes, my bright, entranced, fixed on non-sight
Distance, to which I gain no entrance, seize
My soul. Her mouth dimples bloom-cheeks with tight
Secret private smile. All I do is freeze.
There is a quirky tension in my eyes
And lips; breathing deflates to breathless hush;
The whole world stands still, waits, silently sighs,
Waits waits waits; her sole change – heightening blush.
Still unaware her eyes dilate then flick
Wide open, head shakes; transparent blinds rush
Upwards, leaving her to stare, share a quick
Smile, then apologize with finger-brush.
Fall in love with each other? Should we think?
Sorry, it's too late. We're over the brink.

Sonnet IV
(Wild Song)

Over the years I, Robert Peel, have written
Down matters of the heart in sonnets so,
At this late stage (through with love I thought), smitten
By her youthful beauty, I have a go
At penning impossible dreams the only
Way I know may control such dangerous wild
Bursts of swansongs by me this aging lonely
Poet; that is, to use fourteen lines styled
Into tight (yet I'm rambling) structured form.
Tie me down, for flights of fancy are freaking
Out to break me, as well as to deform
Quiet innocence engaging in seeking.
No future, blood-flame dies down, short of air
This sonnet-run must be a brief affair.

Sonnet V
(Two Hearts)

It was replayed, a Matissean hole-
To-the-heart Icarus painting: heart glowing
With ambition, flight of freedom, free soul,
Love and youth, amid flares of sun, not knowing
Caution – that boring constraint of age. Doomed
To fail, the throbbing heart became a bloody
One that tumbled into the sea entombed
In disappointment leaving fuddy-duddy
Me? I'm not Icarus; fancy love was.
My wholehearted clear sky sweep, Matisse,
Frantic yet tempered, is worth it because
Despite dismantled wing crash I'm in peace.
What's right about this, my flight is unknown.
No harm done. Hurt and gain are mine alone.

Sonnet VI
(Mantles)

Her face mantles and so dismantles my heart.

I catch my breath with extra faint feather beat.

Catchy phrases and metaphors now start

To rush round my snatchy mind to compete

For the honour to describe....O go to hell!

She wants no aids. Her purely natural glow

Requires no artificial make-up. Well,

Does it? Would it not destroy bloom's full blow?

Blow me down I cannot stand any more

Hard made-up beauticians swanning about

Telling pliant clients they're fully sure

Manufactured art would make them stand out.

As my silent adoration stands apart,

Her face mantles and so dismantles my heart.

I normally do not explain anything in my work unless I use a foreign word. However, in this case, the one word is too precious and important not to be comprehended. Of course, one should always have a decent dictionary close to hand. I wonder how many of you know the meaning of "to mantle". In this context, it means for a face "to glow with a blush" (verb intransitive).

Sonnet VII
("Each neate Niplet of her breast")

If a clergyman centuries ago
Could write about "neate niplets", so can I.
I'll shun comparisons with flowers though
Or fruit or gems. I tried to say goodbye
To her ecstasy as she cried, "I must
Keep away from your lovely hands." Yet there
She was, expanding her tight little bust
Even harder, making us more aware.
Do I press the point too much you may ask.
Perhaps I do, perhaps I should retreat,
Lay off, and return to my former task
To write of nipples, ruby red and neat.
Truly they are fine enough to behold
Taste and feel, but most of all, be extolled.

Sonnet VIII
(Over Time)

Over time she has transported me through

Heaven so achingly intense in light

And colours; ubiquitous ruby, blue,

Mauve, pale rose and hints of green all excite.

Now she pulls me dragging lost youth through skies

So terrifying in their unknown black

Stretches of undercurrent where jet cries

Reverberate in lost hearts and wings. Back

Down, I tell myself, let go. You can't suck

Her down into this. It's you who must rush

The abyss to crash. She's just a loon-struck

Girl, after all, with temporary crush.

Injured but relieved I gannet the sea.

Twinged by acute fleeting loss, she flies free.

Sonnet IX
(Half Eighteen)

I aimed to write about my cutest buds

Of May, when dear Shakespeare raised his smooth-bore

Hoary old head and said, "Ye shoot out floods

Of words, yet I have writ it all before."

I reeled to realize eighteen was twice

As many as my nine, but really what

Does it mean? Nothing. My shoots are as nice

In their own way, and the bard is spent shot.

My dearest buds of May, priceless beyond

Aspects of a summer's day, must be praised,

Through multiple meanings; and I respond,

Hand on heart, neither buds nor I are fazed.

Summer will not fade is Will Shakespeare's claim.

To save hawthorn days is Robert Peel's aim.

Sonnet X
(Come)

Come amble down the disused railway line

Where the heady hawthorn has just burst out

And truly my clearest buds of May shine

With pearly hue, putting strong hearts to rout.

Come with me and share those sure scents drifting

Through the fresh air outwafted by those pretty

Flowers – do not pick -- red white or pink, lifting

Us for a while out of life's nitty gritty.

Come agree with me my friend, that my love

For this melting month of May is not misplaced

That I'm correct in setting it above

The norm, in doing so am not disgraced.

I train all my senses to line the way.

Then hope they will let me gather in May.

Sonnet XI
(A Pity)

Shame, that green meteoric racing flame

Of passion is failing and will now expire

Into an ether of forgetfulness. Shame

That such a phenomenon should lose its fire;

Could not evolve into ethereal steady

Heat of constant love blazing until we die

Instead of the all-consuming destructive heady

Burst of amazing burn-out in night-sky.

Of course, its frantic inception had flared

Through sudden euphoria; I must blame

Irrational optimism, which had dared

Flash above the world only to fade. Shame.

All I say is, ride out the searing grief

It was a trailblazer however brief.

Stroke

Sonnet XII
(Post Stroke, Now Aphasia)

The first stroke had caressed with tender stealthy

Tendril filigrees of chains with thought, bound

In curling misty wreaths painful unhealthy

Progress, could still express my thoughts around.

The second strike I find has held me down

With smothered pillow elusive words, shames

Suffocate cradled head in echo-sound

Echo chambers within hide and seek games.

Now, some twenty eight months along the way,

Rents in fog, painful flaw prisms will allow

Me to fashion sentences that they say

Whatever. Head hurts. Soothe me, stroke my brow.

Vocabulary highbrow makes depression

Sans words, pictures and sounds are pure expression.

GLOSSARY

8.   *Radha-Krishna*: The relationship of Radha and Krishna is the embodiment of love, passion and devotion. Krishna, a Hindu deity is often portrayed in various roles: a god-child, a prankster, a model lover, a divine hero and the Supreme Being. Radha is a young woman, a *gopi* (cow-herd girl) who is Krishna's lover. It is said that she controls Krishna with her love. Krishna enchants the world, but Radha enchants even him. Therefore she is the Supreme Goddess of all deities.

15.   *Rat-ki-rani*; Queen of the Night. White tubular flowers intensely fragrant - sweet but not cloying. Common name – Night blooming jasmine.

18.   Khajuraho (or Khujeraho); has the largest group of medieval Hindu and Jain temples famous for their erotic sculpture.

22.   Urvasi; here it is just a woman's Hindu name.

31.   *Kama's* bow; Kama is the God of Love in Hinduism.

37.   *Saptapadi*; Hindu marriage ceremony around a sacred fire in front of Agnidev (the God of Fire and Marriage). The couple circle the fire seven times reciting vows.

Betel leaf enclosed with lime and areca-nut parings (*paan*). When chewed the saliva in the mouth is stained red.

Kama Dev; see 31. God of Love.

Sita & Ram; In the Hindu epic, Ramayana, Sita, Ram's wife, is especially renowned for her faithfulness.

Sati; (or Suttee) the former practice of a widow burning herself to death on her husband's funeral pyre.

39.   *pipal* tree; or (Bodhi tree) – The Sacred Fig.

52.   Juhu; a suburb of Bombay (or Mumbai) famous for its long stretch of beach.

54.   *Adonai*; Jewish Name of God, "Lord".

Byblos; Phoenician city of Gebal.

56.   *Ami du Coeur*; French, Soulmate.

59.   *Aphrodite*; Greek Goddess of Love.

Adonis; Greek God now often used for a young handsome man.